TEN DAILY NEEDS

FOR a HEALTHIER, HAPPIER LIFE

MELINDA H. CONNOR

D.D. Ph.D. AMP FAM

Other books by Melinda H. Connor

Ten daily needs

See auras

Accessing Truth: Emotion, Intuition and Compassion (book and workbook)

Resonance Modulation: Biofield Basics

Advanced Body Reading

Casetaking for the Energy Practitioner

Professional Practice for the Energy Healing Practitioner

The material contained in this book has been written for informational purposes and is not intended as a substitute for medical advice, nor is it intended to diagnose, treat, cure, or prevent disease. If you have a medical issue or illness, consult a qualified physician.

Published by

ARNICA PRESS
www.ArnicaPress.com

Copyright © 2012, 2025 Melinda H. Connor

Written by Melinda H. Connor

Cover Photo: Shutterstock

Manufactured in the United States of America

ISBN: 978-1-955354-63-9

All rights reserved. No part of this book may be reproduced or transmitted in any form or by any means, electronic or mechanical, including photocopying, recording, or by any information storage and retrieval system, without the prior written permission from the Author. This book may not be AI scraped or utilized in AI processes unless permission in writing is received by the author.

THE DISCLAIMER
PLEASE READ BEFORE READING THE BOOK

The information contained in this book, including ideas, suggestions, exercises, meditations, and other materials, is provided only as general information and is solely intended for your own self-improvement. It is not meant to be a substitute for medical or psychological treatment and does not replace the services of health care professionals. If you experience any emotional distress or physical discomfort using any of ideas, suggestions, exercises, or meditations contained in this book, you are advised to stop and to seek professional care, if appropriate.

Publishing of the information contained in this book is not intended to create a client-therapist or any other type of professional relationship between the reader and the author. The author does not make any warranty, guarantee, or prediction regarding the outcome of an individual using this book for any particular purpose or issue.

You agree to assume and accept full responsibility for any and all risks associated with using any of the ideas, suggestions, exercises, or meditations, described in this book and agree to accept full and complete responsibility for applying what you may learn from reading this book. By continuing to read this book you agree to fully release, indemnify, and hold harmless, the author, and others associated with the publication of this book from any claim or liability and for any damage or injury of whatsoever kind or nature which you may incur arising at any time out of or in relation to your use of the information presented in this book. If any court of law rules that any part of the Disclaimer is invalid, the Disclaimer stands as if those parts were struck out.

**BY CONTINUING TO READ THE BOOK
YOU AGREE TO THE DISCLAIMER**

PLEASE ENJOY THE BOOK AND HAVE FUN!

To Drs. Rustum and Della Roy,

Thank you for the mentoring and the wisdom.
I could not have gotten this far without you.
I am profoundly and deeply grateful.

Blessings,

Melinda

ACKNOWLEDGMENTS

I would like to acknowledge the following individuals for their help and support: Dr. Sergey Sheeley-Sorin for his wonderful foreword. It is very beautiful to have Norm's son write the new foreword when Norm had written the foreword for the original volume.

To Dr. Caitlin Connor and Jeffrey Lacy-Ford for the patience and support that they give their often befuddled parent. Dr. Kendra Gaines, my editor extraordinaire. You make me a better writer.

Dr. Midge Murphy and Betsy Lehrfeld, Esq who endeavor to keep me from making legal mistakes. And finally, Sabrina Mesko of Arnica Publishing for her wisdom, patience and amazing artistic eye. I am grateful to all of you.

FOREWORD
BY DR. SERGEY LEO SHEALY-SORIN, MD

Having developed my understanding of whole person healing from the foundation given by my father and guru, Dr. Norm Shealy, MD, the man who is a founding father of Holistic Medicine in the United States and continuing the legacy of holism: a unified spirit, soul, mind and body, it is an honor to work with individual such as Melinda.

A human is more than a collection of molecules. We are more than a bunch of organs put together, and it is truly spirit, soul, mind and body, including feelings, emotions, environment, epigenetics, that creates who we are. In other words, our actions affect and change our genetics, our body, ourselves. The human has incredible power to regenerate, Heal, be happy, healthy. Only specific things are needed consistently, just like plants need watering, sunlight and the correct soil. Like the plants, it is the right combination of factors that support who we are and allow us to be our best.

Dr Mellinda Connor does a wonderful job in a very interactive way, to allow a person to understand, improve, and optimize the required factors for a healthy and happy human life.

It is an honor and a pleasure to know her, work with her and to support her in the truth of her work and in this process.

Blessings,

Dr. Sergey Leo Shealy-Sorin, MD.

Dr. Sergey Leo Shealy-Sorin, M.D. DABFM, holds the title of Medical Director at the esteemed Shealy-Sorin Wellness Institute. He is committed to upholding the legacy of his legally adopted father, the renowned Dr. Norm C. Shealy, "Father of Holistic Medicine," who retired on his 90th birthday in December 2022.

Dr. S has dedicated his life's work to carrying forward the mantle of holistic healing. Hailing from a lineage of medical pioneers, Dr. S had always envisioned himself as a healer, yet his journey took a drastic turn when he was diagnosed with colon cancer in 2007, a brush with fate that would forever transform his understanding of medical practice. Despite the odds, Dr. S emerged from this encounter with an unwavering commitment to holistic healing, and a passion for empowering others to take control of their well-being.

He was named Top Doctor of the Year in Holistic Medicine by the International Association of Top Professionals in 2021. He has an advanced certificate in Health Care Management and has served as a Medical Director at several organizations, including the Bath, NY VA Hospital. With more than 25 years in the industry, his areas of expertise include Urgent Care, Occupational Medicine, and Emergency Medicine, with a holistic approach to pain management, anxiety, depression, chronic disease management, general wellness, hormone therapy, anti-aging, and regenerative medicine.

www.realholisticdoc.com/holistic-healthcare-professionals

FOREWORD BY
C. Norman Shealy, M.D., Ph.D.

Many of us are familiar with Abraham Maslow's hierarchy of needs: physiological, safety, love and belonging, esteem, self- actualization and self-transcendence. Certainly, the basic needs of air, water, food, clothing and shelter are essentials for minimal survival. Dr. Connor includes these in physical environment and feeding of basic needs, to which she adds stable finances—an obvious need to supply these basics!. She covers well love and belonging with her feeling of competence, love connection and level of honor. These are critically essential for self-esteem.

Her 6th needs places some essential "boundaries" on compassion. Otherwise, one may become a rescuer doormat for those who are sappers or zappers. And to keep enthusiasm and excitement she adds learning something new. And of course, integrating this new information into life awakens our most basic human need to be stimulated and to learn from this stimulation.

Finally, her concept of service to the community of the Earth as a whole fulfills what I believe is the most instinctual need of all—to help others. Indeed, as the Urantia Book says, "Love is the desire to do good to others." And when we are helping others, we are fulfilling our most basic spiritual yearnings. However, as she so aptly points out, spirituality is well beyond feeling good about doing good!

Indeed, to me spirituality leads to mysticism—the search for God and the divine. It often begins with spontaneous awareness of the intrinsic beauty of nature. And our awe at the magnificence of our natural world is reinforced by art, music, poetry and great human creations.

To a great extent our 10 daily needs are the broad 10 Commandments of Health.

C. Norman Shealy, M.D., Ph.D.
C. Norman Shealy, M.D., Ph.D.
President, Holos Institutes of Health
Professor Emeritus of Energy Medicine
President Emeritus Holos University Graduate Seminary

Table of Contents

Disclaimer 5
Acknowledgments 9
Foreword by Dr. Sergey Leo Shealy-Sorin, MD 11
Foreword by C. Norman Shealy, M.D., Ph.D. 13

Introduction 19

CHAPTER ONE ~
What is Health? 21
Emotion 24
Thought 25
Trauma 25
Chemistry 26
Genetic predisposition 27
Patterned Re-enforcers 28
Environmental Factors 29
Acoustics 29
Light 30
Spiritual Connection 31

CHAPTER TWO ~
What is Happiness? 33

CHAPTER THREE ~

Does Your Life Work? 37
Thought 38
Emotion 39
Trauma 39
Genetic Predisposition 39
Patterned reinforcement 40
Physics 40
Acoustics 40
Light 41
Chemistry 41
Environment 41
Spiritual Connection 41

CHAPTER FOUR ~

Healthy Life Elements 43
    1. Physical Environment 43
    2. Feeding of Basic Needs 45
    3. Feeling of competence at something 46
    4. Some love connection 47
    5. Some level of honor 48
    6. Compassion with Boundaries! 49
    7. Learning something new 51
    8. Integrating new information into your life 51
    9. Service to the community of the Earth 52
    10. An act of Spirituality 53

CHAPTER FIVE ~
Assessing Your Life State 55
Task One 55
Task Two 56
Task Three 57
Task Four 57
Task Five 58
Meditations 58
    1. Physical Environment.. 59
    2. Feeding of Basic Needs 59
    3. Feeling of Competence at Something 60
    4. Some Love Connection 61
    5. Some Level of Honor 62
    6. Compassion With Boundaries... 63
    7. Learning Something New 63
    8. Integrating New Information into Your Life 65
    9. Service to the Community of the Earth as a Whole ... 65
    10. Spirituality.. 66

CHAPTER SIX ~
Need for Support 69

CHAPTER SEVEN ~
Internal and External Resistance 73

CHAPTER EIGHT ~
Possibility of Change 77

CHAPTER NINE ~
Advance Planning !..81
Selection of Which Change to Make 82
Planning, Implementation, and the Doing! 82
What information do I need? 83
Language and the Process 84
Friends and Family 85
Work and the Changes 86
Resistance to Change 87
Integration, De-integration and the New you 87

CHAPTER TEN ~
No guilt – The restart! 89

CHAPTER ELEVEN ~
The next day of Your Life 93

About the Author..95

Introduction

In the re-birthing of this book fifteen years after the original edition, I ended up reflecting on how people have used the book and their feedback. I have been deeply gratified by the emails and phone calls of people who found this information valuable. It has been equally as valuable a process for me.

Taking stock at this time and looking at all the feedback has allowed me to notice where in my own life I am not "walking my talk." I invite readers into a journey of self-assessment and self-reflection as you read. Make a list of things that do not work yet in your life. Pick at least one and make a start. It becomes a new and fresh start to a new and fresh way of being.

I also want to say a special thank you to Sergey for doing the new forward. We have known each other for over twenty years and have worked on various projects and research together over that time. He has a schedule that is even heavier than mine, and I am deeply gratified that he has taken the time to add his wisdom to this book by writing the new forward. It, too, brings a fresh start to the process of self-discovery.

So now, let us begin!

What are the components necessary for a healthier, happier life?

1. **Physical Environment**
   (shelter, physical safety, physical health)

2. **Feeding of basic needs**
   (food, water, stable finances)

3. **Feeling of competence at something**

4. **Some love connection**

5. **Some level of honor**

6. **Compassion with boundaries**

7. **Learning something new**

8. **Integrating new information**

9. **Service to the Community of the Earth as a Whole**

10. **Spirituality**

CHAPTER ONE

WHAT IS HEALTH?

Health is a combination of factors that in the end have you feeling good. You feel good about your body. You feel like your body can meet your daily needs. Health is about a body that has a reasonable level of fitness. Health is about a body that is free of pain and disease. Health is about a body that fits your life and your lifestyle. Health includes all aspects of being. Your physical body is not the sum of what it means to be healthy. Instead your mind and your spirit are included in your health. It is an integrated form of body, mind and spirit that creates health.

A person's definition of health changes in different parts of their life journey. When you are 20 and like to run six miles four times a week, you may have one definition of health. That definition would include being able to do the run comfortably, freely and in a reasonable period of time. When you are 50 you may be doing a different run or a different type of exercise. I did yoga in my 50's instead of regular running so that I had a different kind of stress on my joints. Yoga felt more comfortable to me and I felt healthier when I did it. I also pay attention to nutrition in a way that I did not in my fast food junky days of my 20's. At 70 I like to ride horses, as moving joints more subtly is gentler on my body and still includes stretching.

A person's definition of health is also different for each sex. A man who is very physically fit in his 20's may really enjoy football and practice on a regular basis. He may or may not be nutrition conscious and enjoy hiking and white water rafting.

A woman may enjoy those things as well but often she will choose a slightly different range of activities. For example: a woman might go to a step class at her local gym and swim three mornings a week. She might pay attention to her weight but not be as careful about fad diets. When I was in my 20's, a one-ton delivery of 100-pound bales of hay was not a big deal to put into the barn. In my 50's most of the men I know are stronger than I am, and I am very happy to have their help putting hay into the barn.

Health can also be specific for a group. For example: I have a friend my age who likes to square dance. She and her husband are very fit! But they do a great deal of traveling with their dancing and that can have impact on their health. Though I love square dancing, I prefer to spend my exercise time doing ballet and yoga and spend more of my time with a like-minded group of individuals. I find that my yoga friends, instead of dealing with a busy travel schedule, are very nutrition conscious and their focus on nutrition has a positive impact on their health.

People in different parts of the country and in different parts of the world can have different definitions of what it is to be healthy too. For example: when I lived in New England in the winter, running outside in the snow and on the ice was not my most favorite experience. My definition of health in those days was to make it through a winter without bronchitis! Now I live in southern Arizona and my definition of health includes not getting heat stroke in the summer when I do ranch work. If I were a woman in an area of the world where I would need to be able to carry a heavy water jar on my head each day, my definition of health would include a strong neck and shoulders. So, health can vary based on location and the specific needs of the individuals living in that area.

> **WHAT IS HEALTH?**
>
> **IT IS ABOUT AN INTEGRATED FORM OF FEELING GOOD WHICH INCLUDES BODY, MIND AND SPIRIT.**
>
> **IT IS DIFFERENT FOR DIFFERENT STAGES OF THE LIFE JOURNEY.**
>
> **IT IS DIFFERENT FOR EACH SEX.**
>
> **IT IS DIFFERENT WITHIN ANY SINGLE GROUP.**
>
> **IT IS DIFFERENT FOR EACH PART OF THE WORLD.**

Emotion

As you can see, health is actually a dance of factors. The universe is a very creative place. For example, health includes your emotional state because that affects the biochemistry of your body and your brain. Emotional responses are in part a result of hormones generated by your own body. Remember all those stories about women who are pregnant and cry at the drop of a hat?

Well, that is the result of all those changes in the hormonal system during pregnancy. Most people do not realize that our hormones change on a daily, weekly and monthly basis. For example, what has been called the "stress hormone," cortisol, has a normal 24-hour cycle. It is higher first thing in the morning and during the day and then it goes lower at night so that you can sleep.

When your emotions are out of balance because of stressors in your life the situation acts as a complication. If you are feeling down, it can be harder to get things done. It can be more difficult to organize and accomplish tasks. So, paying attention to you emotional state can impact how healthy and happy you are day to day.

THOUGHT

Health includes how you think, what you think, how the thoughts are moving through your brain and how they are connecting to your neurological system. My grandmother used to say "Thoughts have weight, so you need to be sure they do not get too heavy." By that she was saying to me that I needed to manage my thoughts. I needed to notice if they were repetitive, if they were negative and if they were dark and angry.

Repetitive thoughts can cause you to burn through your healthy brain chemicals faster than you should. One of the easy things to do is to notice. If you are thinking a negative thought, hearing a phrase over and over in your head, you probably need to interrupt it. What is a positive spin that you could give the thought? What could you be thinking that would bring value to you and to those around you instead?

TRAUMA

Trauma has an impact on health. It includes both physical and emotional trauma. And trauma doesn't have to be big or bold. It can be a repetitive type trauma. If you have seen somebody play the violin you will have noticed that there's a vibrato tremolo that they do with the wrist to do their bowing work. That type of movement over time can cause a repetitive injury.

Today, many people have not put their bodies in the correct position to do computer work without causing repetitive injuries. Carpel tunnel type injuries can be caused by the stress of sitting and typing hour after hour with your body in the wrong position. Once you are injured it can limit what you can do in the future. Why have stress or repetitive injuries happen to you? Instead, be proactive and act in favor of health! Think about your daily life. Are there movement patterns which you are doing again and again during your day? What type of movement? Do you need to have your position as you're doing that movement checked to see if you are in a relaxed position? What about getting exercises from a physical therapist or exercise physiologist to balance those movements? Consider taking action in your life to help you move toward and maintain your health in this area.

Chemistry

Chemistry is a factor in health. It will impact your life in lots of different ways. You have body chemistry. You have chemicals that you put on your body. You have chemicals that you put in your body. You have chemicals that you have in your environment. All of these types of chemicals impact your body on a daily basis and you may not be aware of the impact.

One of the biggest areas where chemistry impacts your life is in your nutrition. You have heard the phrase, "You are what you eat." It is true. Your body is only going to be as healthy as the nutrition you put into it. You have to have the right kind of nutrition for your body. It needs to be clean food and it needs to be food that your body can absorb.

When I work with clients to support their movement back toward health I always refer to a qualified nutritionist as part of the process. Simple easy changes to your diet can make a major difference in how you feel. I used to be the queen of fast food but shifting to healthy eating habits gave me more energy and gave me a more positive outlook day to day. I can now actively tell the difference when I have eaten something that is not life supporting. I feel it almost immediately. So consider a nutritional consult and a move toward healthy eating.

Genetic Predisposition

We all have genes. Those genes help to pick our hair and eye color. They help us to be taller or shorter. They affect the taste of food that we eat and how well our body processes those foods.

Have you ever noticed that while family members can have the same basic genetic structure, only some of the family members will have a particular issue? I have long been fascinated with why only some members of a family will have genetic issues manifest. No one knows that answer but there are some very practical things that you can do to help yourself if there is a genetic issue for your family. First, understand the issue and what research information is available. Next, put a plan in place to keep yourself as healthy as possible. Finally, live your life with the expectation that you will be healthy. Worrying about anything stresses the body. So do good things for yourself, live sensibly and have a great time instead.

PATTERNED RE-ENFORCERS

You can have patterned re-enforcers, something that you do habitually, the way that you put a foot down, the way that you sit, the way that you move from one thing to another, both physically and emotionally. You can have habitual patterns that can cause repetitive injury type syndromes. You can have the actual physics of a situation be correct or incorrect for your body. My daughter went to the shoe store where she was going to get herself a pair of high heels for the prom. We got a pair of absolutely stunning high heels that are horrific for your feet and we had a very, very long talk after she wore them for about 20 minutes at home to break them in and discovered she was in agony.

Patterned re-enforcers can also be emotional or behavioral. If you spend a moment thinking you may be able to remember a behavior that you have done that another family member has done as well. When I was about twelve my mother was nagging me about something and suddenly burst out laughing. She said, "I sound just like my mother!" When my daughter was about the same age I found myself saying the exact words my mother had said to me. Those words had traveled three generations.

Environmental Factors

You can have environmental factors that make a direct impact and environmental factors come in all sorts of different forms. How many people work on laptops? How many people have the screen when you're in a regular environment up high enough so that your eyes are mid-level in the screen? It is very unusual to have it in the correct position. Congratulations to those of you who are in the correct position. Most of us are bent over, with rolled shoulders, neck stretching down, putting pressure on the elbows and putting pressure on the first ribs. It becomes an issue for your body over time.

You can have environmental type stressors when you're doing the various kinds of work. Sound in many work environments can be a challenge. So can the quality of air in many large buildings. The area you drive through going to and from work, which may have a high level of exhaust can have an impact on your body. Environmental stressors of many kinds can have a continuing impact on your health.

Acoustics

Acoustics make a difference to your body. How many of you have had teenagers or lived around teenagers and had to deal the "let's take the sound and crank it up as far as it can go"? My daughter is very into her music. She loves to sing and sing out so when she cranks a stereo up it truly makes the windows rattle in the house. That volume of sound actually can cause tissue stress and damage on your physical tissue structures if you're listening to it a long time. It does more than affect your hearing but impacts every tissue in the body. Dr. Ann Baldwin at the University of Arizona looked at sound stress on tissue with rats and found that it affected how well the body can absorb nutrients. Sound stress caused the intestines to tear and leak. So you may want to pay attention to the volume of sound which is around you.

Light

Light is a factor, and it turns out it is a very, very major factor in health. It turns out that we have to have blue light, both in the visual range and in the non-visual range, and if you don't have blue light your brain doesn't function. You can't think correctly. So the light became absolutely important. Seasonal affective disorder is directly related to how much light you are getting. If you do not get enough light of the right kinds you can become depressed. It turns out that when people are working in cubicles where there is no direct sunlight, they're not going to be as efficient.

People must have contact with direct sunlight to help their brains to work. This is very important in northern climates where it becomes dark earlier in the day and it stays dark longer in the mornings. If you get in that situation where you're getting up in the dark, you're going home in the dark, you're in a cubicle inside an office building and you're not getting enough of these blue light frequencies, then your brain stops working as effectively. You can supplement with full spectrum lighting and many businesses in this country have made the change to full spectrum lights because it is just good business to have people who can work at full capacity.

SPIRITUAL CONNECTION

Our bodies need a spiritual connection. In fact it turns out that our brains are hardwired for spirituality. Spiritual acts release a chemical called dopamine into the brain. Dopamine helps manage your muscles so that they can move smoothly and it also helps us to feel good. So spiritual actions help create a positive brain response. For our purpose there is a distinction between religion and spirituality. A spiritual act can be listening to a beautiful piece of music. A spiritual act can be walking in a wonderful woodland area. A spiritual act can be sitting and watching a sun set.

> **HEALTH IS IMPACTED BY LOTS OF FACTORS THAT CAN INCLUDE:**
>
> **THOUGHT   EMOTION   TRAUMA**
> **PHYSICS   ACOUSTICS   LIGHT**
> **CHEMISTRY   ENVIRONMENT**
>
> **SPIRITUAL CONNECTION**
> **GENETIC PREDISPOSITION**
> **PATTERNED REINFORCEMENT**

All of these many factors have an impact on your health. They impact your daily life and can impact your perspective on your life. Recognizing which of these factors most directly impact your life in a positive or negative way can help you to change your life for the better.

CHAPTER TWO

WHAT IS HAPPINESS?

What is happiness? Happiness is a very organic process and it actually turns out that it's unique to each individual and is a biochemical reaction to a physical or emotional stimulus. Happiness actually changes your brain chemistry. When you're happy there's a cascade effect that happens throughout the endocrine system. It's really lovely for your body. Joy. Love. Laughter. All of these have a place in happiness. Love can create a state of happiness. Doing work that you love can create happiness. And it is your individual experience of the process that defines your experience of that happy state.

Happiness can also be the result of a change in individual perception. Sometimes you can be in a place where if you reframe what you're thinking about, reshape it, reorganize it, you can look at something that originally was a drain and a strain and aggravation and it becomes an opportunity. It may be an opportunity to make a change. It may be an opportunity to shift so that you feel like so that you are more in tune.

Happiness can also be the result of a new experience. When you try something new it's really cool and it's really exciting. The very first time I did a ropes course, I was so excited and so happy when I succeeded at walking across the rope. It was great! So that opportunity to challenge yourself with that new experience can take and shift how you're functioning and what you're doing. Happiness really is an art because it's unique for you and to you. Because our bodies are all unique, an individual work of art, all of us will have a definition that is organic to ourselves.

> **WHAT IS HAPPINESS?**
>
> **A BIOCHEMICAL REACTION TO A PHYSICAL OR EMOTIONAL STIMULUS.**
>
> **A CHANGE IN INDIVIDUAL PERCEPTION.**
>
> **AN OPPORTUNITY FOR A NEW EXPERIENCE.**
>
> **AN ART!**

Why would people want to be happy and healthy? Because it feels good! When you feel good it makes your life better. Things start to work.

Being ill can be really challenging and it doesn't have to be a major illness. I was working on the computer a couple of days ago and I got a paper cut on the end of my finger where I have to type. It hurt every single time I put my finger on a key. Illness does not have to be huge. It can just be something that simple that's an aggravation and is challenging. It changes the rhythm of your work and your life.

Being unhappy has an impact on everybody around you. It changes the way you make contact with people. It changes the kind of space that you need, the dialogue that you're doing with people, and how things flow from Point A to Point B. It can affect your ability to work successfully. I did not type well the day I got the paper cut and I didn't get half of what I normally get done completed. It had direct impact on the rest of that weekend.

Illness or injury of any kind has a direct effect on relationships. It can make them stronger as you work together to create a positive situation. Or it can weaken and perhaps destroy relationships. It is possible to create a positive effect from any illness but recognizing the opportunity for change and taking full advantage of those opportunities is an important part of creating that positive effect.

> **WHY DO PEOPLE WANT TO BE HEALTHY AND HAPPY?**
>
> **BEING ILL CAN BE VERY CHALLENGING. BEING UNHAPPY AFFECTS ALL THE PEOPLE AROUND YOU.**
>
> **IT CAN AFFECT YOUR ABILITY TO WORK SUCCESSFULLY.**
>
> **RELATIONSHIPS CHANGE IN MANY WAYS.**

CHAPTER THREE

DOES YOUR LIFE WORK?

This is a really important question. Does your life work? Be honest with yourself. If you can say yes, then you're in pretty good shape and you can just read the rest of the book for fun and information. If you can say, "well, sort of," then hopefully some of this will help and it may be time to explore the additional information. If the answer is no, it is time to make some changes and get back on track. If you are healthy you act in support of everyone around you in part by example. If you are happy, it rubs off on everyone with whom you come in contact.

Have you noticed when you are happy how people smile around you? Isn't that lovely when they smile? A smile is a positive experience that keeps giving to more than just you.

So to isolate the areas that are not working as well, let's look at each of the components to health that we have mentioned in chapters 1 and 2. Below are a series of questions to help you focus on one or more areas where you might like to see change.

THOUGHT

Do you have repetitive thoughts? If yes, are those positive or negative? Do you think angry or aggressive thoughts at frequent intervals throughout your day? When you are thinking, do you focus on the negative aspects of your life? Are you able to focus your thoughts or does your mind wander? Do you have any trouble remembering information? Do you have any trouble organizing information?

If the answer is yes to any of these questions, this may be an area that you wish to explore more fully.

> **HAVE YOU LOOKED AT ENVIRONMENTAL FACTORS?**
>
> **ARE THE BASIC LIFE REQUIREMENTS IN PLACE?**
> **(LAUNDRY, BILLS, HOUSING...)**
>
> **ARE HEALTHY LIFE FACTORS ALL IN GOOD SHAPE?**
>
> **DO YOU NEED A PSYCHOLOGICAL ASSESSMENT OR TUNE-UP?**
>
> **WHEN WAS YOUR LAST PHYSICAL ASSESSMENT?**

Emotion

Do you feel burnt-out? Do you feel emotionally tired all the time? Does it feel like you cry about everything? Do you have significant mood swings? Do you feel angry much of the time? Do you feel sad or despairing much of the time? Do your emotional responses get in the way of your daily life or your work life? Do you feel that you cannot make contact with another person? Do you feel that there is no one to love you?

If the answer is yes to any of these questions this may be an area that you wish to explore more fully.

Trauma

Have you experienced a physical, emotional or spiritual trauma in recent years? Do you have movement patterns that could be causing repetitive patterns? Do you have an injury pattern that has repeated itself?

If the answer is yes to any of these questions, this may be an area that you wish to explore more fully.

Genetic Predisposition

Are there genetic issues for your family that you are aware of and that you worry about? Have you seen a TV special or read something on the web that sounds like a physical issue with which you have been dealing?

If the answer is yes to any of these questions, this may be an area that you wish to explore more fully.

PATTERNED REINFORCEMENT

Do you find that words that your parents said are coming out of your mouth? Do you find you are doing behaviors again and again, even when you do not like those behaviors? Do you find that you have difficulty implementing changes in your life?

If the answer is yes to any of these questions, this may be an area that you wish to explore more fully.

PHYSICS

Is your body tired and achy after a day at work because of the body position you are holding? Do you forget to stretch and move every few hours as you work? Do you have to carry things that are particularly heavy on a regular basis and end up achy because of it?

If the answer is yes to any of these questions this may be an area that you wish to explore more fully.

ACOUSTICS

Are you always turning the sound up on the TV, radio, computer etc? Do your ears ring for hours at a time? Do you feel exhausted after listening to people talk? Does your body feel like it is vibrating after you get home from work because the sound level was so high?

If the answer is yes to any of these questions, this may be an area that you wish to explore more fully.

Light

Do you feel as if you never see daylight? Do you feel as if the rooms you are in are too dark? When you go outside, does it feel too bright? Do you have to blink away tears when you go outside because the light is so bright? Do you feel constantly tired and a bit depressed in the winter?
If the answer is yes to any of these questions, this may be an area that you wish to explore more fully.

Chemistry

Do you eat well? Do you eat foods that are correct and nutritionally balanced for your body? Do you know enough about nutrition to support your health?
If the answer is no to any of these questions, this may be an area that you wish to explore more fully.

Environment

Do you live in a physically safe and healthy environment? Do you work in a safe environment? Are you free from significant environmental stressors in the area where you live? When you travel to and from work or daily activities, do you travel in an area that is safe environmentally?
If the answer is no to any of these questions, this may be an area that you wish to explore more fully.

Spiritual Connection

Do you feel connected spiritually? Do you have regular and daily spiritual experiences? Do you take time for meditation or contemplation? Do you know what your purpose is in life?

If the answer is no to any of these questions, this may be an area that you wish to explore more fully.

Though each of these areas can overlap, you will want to pick just one area on which to focus. Once you have a general area to look at, then you will want to go to the next level. What are the life elements that need to be in place for your life to work, and how do these life elements apply to the area that you have picked? Why are these life elements so important? We will take a look at this part of the process next.

CHAPTER FOUR

HEALTHY LIFE ELEMENTS

So what are the kinds of analysis that you have to do to see where your life is and whether or not your life is working? Let's go through the basic factors that need to be included every 24 hours and talk about them in a little more detail. As we do this, I would like you to begin to think about the various areas of your life that we are discussing. Just notice for now if that area of your life is working.

NUMBER 1: PHYSICAL ENVIRONMENT

The first factor is physical and environmental. You need to have a healthy life environment. So the very first question to ask yourself is, "Do I have a safe space for downtime?" Every 24 hours your body has to have time to down-regulate your brain and let it relax. If that period of rest and relaxation does not happen or does not happen in a safe space, the brain changes and cannot function properly.

What about chemicals that smell or that pollute your local environment? If you live in a major city you may be having issues with lead poisoning or carbon monoxide from car exhaust and not be aware of it. There are inexpensive detectors that you can get at the local hardware store to be sure that this is not an issue in your local space.

If you are living in a high rise apartment you may not be getting enough good quality oxygen. You may want to check and see just how much oxygen is making it up to your apartment.

When you are looking at a safe physical space you can have organic things that show up. For example, in many homes in Colorado there's a huge issue with radon in basements. In Northern Arizona there's a problem with arsenic in the ground. It's actually physically part of the ground substructure and if you drill a well you may be drilling down through the layer that contains the arsenic.

Many city water supplies are treated with chemicals on a regular basis. While those chemicals do not affect most people, and are often necessary to maintain the water quality, there are some individuals who are sensitive to them. You can have your water tested by a private company quickly and easily to determine if this is an issue in your area.

Many electric companies are switching to microwave based smart meters. If you have a smart meter on your house you may want to consider shielding to protect people within the household. At the very least you will want to make sure that no one is sleeping with a 10-12 foot range of the meters.

These kinds of physical environmental factors can actually have a fair amount of impact on your health. Simple fixes can make sure that you have a safe and protected environment in which to have rest time.

NUMBER 2: FEEDING OF BASIC NEEDS

It is very important that all of your healthy life factors are in place. These healthy life factors include things like: rest, proper exercise, healthy food, enough clean water to drink, daily mechanics support and a stable financial situation.

You may want to consider the following questions: Do you need some sort of a psychological tune-up? Do you have an area where you may need support in your life? Are you in a transition process or in an organic creation process and you just need somebody to listen to your ideas? Is your body where it needs to be? Do you need to develop an exercise program that fits you and your life?

Do you drink enough water? Most Americans don't drink enough water. Seventy to 80 percent of Americans are chronically dehydrated. If your lips have any cracking at all, you're dehydrated.

And be sure to look at the question of stable finances because it can change. You can be very stable but be in the process of buying or selling a home and during that period things can be unstable.

Daily mechanics are part of the basic life requirements. If they are not properly in place, it is amazing how the basics can be a tremendous aggravation. I live out in the middle of the desert. There are no services out here. There's no gas station, no 7-Eleven, no shopping centers, and I have to do dry cleaning of business suits and professional attire on a regular basis. It is nine miles to the closest gas station. I had a real problem because I could not get to the dry cleaner except in the morning. The fact that they closed before I could get there in the afternoons became a huge aggravation. What about trying to get five loads of laundry done each day? Getting the dishes done each evening? Vacuuming? Scrubbing the bathroom? When you are working, staying on top of some of these daily mechanics becomes a real chore. Take a moment to look at each of these issues and see if any one of them is a stressor.

NUMBER 3: FEELING OF COMPETENCE AT SOMETHING

A feeling of competence at something is a very important aspect of our lives. How many of us put a bar at one place and then when we meet it we look at it and we say, "Oh I think the bar should be higher"? How many of us take the beat pause before we raise the bar and say, "I met the bar and I did a good job"? Did you know that your brain chemistry changes when you pat yourself on the back? We call it a "beat pause" because ordinarily we just raise the bar really, really fast and we don't stop, to give ourselves credit for the good that we have done during the day. Oh, I did this. Okay, it's here. And it happens about that fast. You need that beat pause to honor the self.

It is common in our society to focus on the negative, on everything that went wrong or that you felt you did wrong that day. You have to give equal time to the things you did well. You may not be a leader in every area of your life, but for good brain health it is useful to have at least one area where you feel as if you are contributing in a positive way. If you do not have that one aspect you need to find and develop an area of interest and passion. Then you need to develop competence in that area so that you can allow yourself to feel satisfaction.

So right now take just a minute and take a breath and acknowledge to yourself something that you did successfully today.

Number 4: Some love connection

One day I came home from high school and was in that state of true teenage angst. I had just broken up with my boyfriend of the moment and life as we knew it was over. I was crushed in only the way a teenager can be. One of my mother's friends was over visiting and he was one of the kindest and most profoundly wise men I have ever known in my life. He's passed away now, but he was a glorious human being and that day he said to me, "Melinda, for true love and affection, sometimes there ain't nothin' like a good dog."

Everyone needs a love connection and everyone needs regular physical touching. The touch needs to be human but it does not have to be sexual. The love part does not have to be human. I think that dogs know more about how to love the world and people in the world than humans do at this time. They do "I'm a happy person" and "I love the world, did you smell that rabbit?" really, really well. Many dogs are just so bright and so happy and so full of personality, it just lifts your heart.

The love connection doesn't necessarily have to be an intimate relationship type connection, though that's very beautiful; it can also be a relationship between good friends. It can be a relationship between sisters or brothers. It can be a relationship between cousins. So it can come from many, many different places so that the nurturing happens and that love connection is there.

Physical touch is something that humans need to survive. Babies who are not touched die. The touch needs to be appropriate to the situation and circumstances of those involved. Getting regular physical touch in the form of a hug from a friend, a gentle massage, or a pat on the hand from your aunt Clara can be very reassuring and nurturing.

Number 5: Some level of honor

One of the surprising things that we discovered as we did research on the brain was that people who commit an honorable act on a regular basis have their brain chemistry working in the correct direction. The body actually needs you to honor yourself and to have honor in something that you're doing on a daily basis. Acts that are honorable support the production of serotonin which is a chemical that is good for brain health.

It does not have to be a dramatic and large act. For example, somebody left change on my desk the other day. We had gone to lunch together and they made sure I got it back. It can be leaving the correct tip for the waitress. It can be admitting that you forgot to get something done and taking care to get it done. Simple things. It doesn't have to be dramatic.

It is also ethics and ethical behavior. You need to feel good about who you are as a person. To feel internally good, you want your personal ethics to be working. Spend a moment right now and check in with your internal barometer. Do you believe that you are living a life that is honorable? Do you believe that your behavior is ethical? Remember, you can take simple actions to keep yourself on the right track.

Number 6: Compassion with Boundaries!

Compassion with boundaries. As my daughter says, "Oh no it's the B word." It can be a tough one. Having appropriate boundaries can be a big challenge when you have hearts that give a lot and care a great deal. Where do you set the boundary that's appropriate? Where is that dance when you say no, it's not okay to go any further?

Compassion is good for the brain. It releases both serotonin and dopamine. It can also affect your endorphins. When you do something compassionate for someone it can make you feel good about yourself. And when was the last time you practiced compassion toward yourself?

The Ten Daily Needs are:

1. **Physical Environment** (shelter, physical safety, physical health)

2. **Feeding of basic needs** (food, water, stable finances)

3. **Feeling of competence at something.**

4. **Some love connection**

5. **Some level of honor**

6. **Compassion with boundaries**

7. **Learning something new**

8. **Integrating new information into your life**

9. **Service to the community of the Earth as a whole**

10. **Spirituality**

Does anything in this picture sound familiar? Have you put in your 90+ hour week? Eaten only fast food? Slept about four hours a night? Not had a chance to exercise and not seen daylight in a week? Perhaps a little compassion toward the self is in order!

NUMBER 7: LEARNING SOMETHING NEW

The ability to learn something new is an important part of body health that goes all the way back to the survival of the fittest. Recently, the *New York Times* newspaper had on the front page a story about the new research showing longevity is increased by learning. How wonderful!

When you are born you have many more nerves in your brain than you do when you die. While it does not work this way all the time it turns out your brain is wired so that you use your nerves in your brain or your brain gets rid of the nerves. It is called neurological pruning. The brain may remap another nerve to do dual duty, but it won't regenerate the nerve that was originally there. So the more active you keep your brain, and the more of your brain you utilize, the healthier your brain is and the better it works.

NUMBER 8: INTEGRATING NEW INFORMATION INTO YOUR LIFE

Another survival of the fittest aspect to your health is the ability to integrate new information back in to your life and your behavior. The body is an oscillating system. Your heart is beating. That's an oscillation. You take a breath.

That's an oscillation. You put your foot down. That's a percussive oscillation. It happens when the waters of the body are shaken and that ability to integrate and make the changes keeps you moving in that nice wave pattern so that you're continually flowing and changing in the moment. Humans are not static. We did not get to the top of the predatory tree by being static.

New information is coming to us all the time and we need to be able to integrate that information into successful survival behaviors. More than survival, new information is fun! Think about the last time you learned and mastered a new skill. Was it fun to be able to do it well? Think about the last time you had a new piece of information that changed how you were doing your work. Did it make your life easier?

What is one thing that you have always wanted to learn? This may be the time to start!

NUMBER 9: SERVICE TO THE COMMUNITY OF THE EARTH AS A WHOLE

The ability to take an altruistic action is one of the best things about our being human. Service to the community of the Earth as a whole is an important part of protecting our world. We are all living on the same planet and we need a world for our children to grow up in and inherit. An altruistic action is also good for your body. Cortisol, which is a stress hormone, can be reduced with altruistic actions. The action can be as simple as putting your cans in for recycling. What did you do today that was altruistic?

Number 10: An act of Spirituality

Spirituality is important to your brain health. It actually turns out that your brain is hard wired for spirituality. Now, for some people that means a religious activity, but it doesn't necessarily have to mean an organized religious activity. It can be walking out on a path in nature and feeling connected to it for a few minutes. It can be sitting and looking at a painting and really understanding what the artist was trying to convey. It can be listening to a beautiful piece of music that connects you to everything around you.

Spiritual experiences are all individual. Spirituality in this context also includes spiritual actions, things like acts of forgiveness and acts of kindness. A spiritual act can involve some of the oldest parts of the brain and keep them stimulated and healthy.

CHAPTER FIVE

ASSESSING YOUR LIFE STATE

So now in your own life, how are you doing? Are there areas where you need a tune-up? Is there some sort of restoration process that you need to go through? You may find as we go through each of the ten areas that there is something you want to change in each area or in several of the areas. Pick one to start and only one. Focus on the one and do an honest, thorough job of assessing your life.

Task One

The first task in this process is to select one of the ten areas to work on. Which of the ten feels like it would be the easiest to change? Start with something simple. Do not pick something big just because you are in a hurry to make lots of changes fast. The reason you are picking something simple the first time is to build your skills. Once you have the skills and understand both the steps and the stressors of the change process, you can challenge yourself with bigger changes. Let yourself be successful. Start with the things that are easier first.

Here are the ten areas again:

1. Physical Environment (shelter, physical safety, physical health)
2. Feeding of basic needs (food, water, stable finances)
3. Feeling of competence at something.
4. Some love connection
5. Some level of honor
6. Compassion with boundaries
7. Learning something new
8. Integrating new information into your life
9. Service to the community of the earth as a whole
10. Spirituality

Remember to pick something that is simple and focused for your first change.

TASK TWO

The second task in this process is to define the problem which you are facing. Write the problem down and see if your definition is exact. A sample problem definition in the basic needs area might look something like:

"I have to get to the dry cleaners twice a week. There are no dry cleaners for 37 miles from my house. I need a dry cleaner that is open from 7am to 7pm at least one day at the beginning of the week and one day at the end of the week. I want them to have reasonable rates and if possible a frequent buyer plan. I want them to be in a safe area of town so that I can be there after dark and not worry. I would like the dry cleaner to be environmentally conscious in their chemical use and in their chemical disposal."

Notice that there are a number of different pieces in the definition. It is an additive process. In the beginning you will want to put in everything that you would like to have included. You may modify or change your requirements as you get information. However, start by listing everything that you want to include.

Task Three

Your third task is to research options that might be available to solve the issue and help you to make the change. Go to the library or online to see what options are available to help you. Take a look in the phone book. What kind of actual resources will you need to accomplish the change? Do an additional search on the internet. Perhaps there are others in your local community who are also looking for a similar change. You will want to spend a little time on the research. You may be surprised at the options that are available to you. Remember, you are focusing on resources to help you make the change and to make it successfully. We will go into the process of getting the correct support more deeply in the next chapter of the book.

Task Four

Task four is to meditate on what you want to create and imagine or vision the end result. Below are a series of meditations for each of the areas involved. These are suggestions and you can certainly write your own. The meditations can also help you to overcome challenges as you make the changes. This gives you time to put all the pieces of the process into perspective and to see if you have missed anything that needs to be done to make you successful.

Task Five

The fifth task is the most fun. Put your change in place and begin enjoying the new you!

Meditations

For each of these meditations you will need a quiet spot to sit. Sit in a way that is comfortable for you. Make sure that your back is properly supported. Wear comfortable clothes. Have water available for you to drink when you finish the meditation. Have a notebook and pen handy to write down flashes of inspiration or insight. Remember this is fun to do. Do not stress about the process. Whatever happens is fine. Spend a maximum of about 20 minutes on the process. You can do any meditation more than once but limit the time you spend in the actual meditation. Most people who do not meditate regularly have difficulty sleeping if they meditate more than 20 minutes in a day. You may want to set an alarm clock to bring you out of the meditation and let you know that time is up. Pick a sound that is not too jarring. You want to come out of the process gradually.

You can also read the meditation into a tape recorder for personal use. Read it slowly and practice the breathing as you read the text so that you will give yourself enough time during the actual meditation. Remember the goal here is change. It is not to become the world's most fabulous meditator.

1. Physical Environment

Sit comfortably in a chair or on a cushion. Take a breath and let it out. Let your body feel the support of the chair. Take another breath and let it out. Begin to feel your seat bones. Take your next breath and take the breath in as if you were breathing from your seat bones. Bring the breath all the way down your body. Let your eyes close and let the feeling of your body just breathing wash over you. Now think about what you want to change. Keep feeling into the area of your seat bones. Breathe in the color cherry red. If you like let yourself imagine what cherry red would taste like and how it would smell. Just be and breathe. Then just watch what images flash by. Do not get involved with them. Just watch. When the images slow down, allow yourself to see the change happening successfully. Let your imagination go and see yourself happy and successful. When you are ready bring yourself back. Take a final cleansing breath. Have a nice drink of water and write down any notes or insights that you may have had during the process.

2. Feeding of Basic Needs

Sit comfortably in a chair or on a cushion. Take a breath and let it out. Let your body feel the support of the chair. Take another breath and let it out. Begin to feel your pelvic area. Take your next breath and take the breath in as if you were breathing from your pelvic area. Bring the breath all the way down your body. Let your eyes close and let the feeling of your body just breathing wash over you. Now think about what you want to change. Keep feeling into the area of your pelvis. Then just watch what images flash by. Do not get involved with them. Just watch. If you start to be overwhelmed pull yourself back a little bit into the now moment. To strengthen this process, let yourself breathe in the color orange. Let your self imagine what it would be like to smell and taste orange as you feel into the pelvic area. Remember, just let the images pass by. When the images slow down, allow yourself to see the change happening successfully. Let your imagination go and see yourself happy and successful. When you are ready bring yourself back. Take a final cleansing breath. Have a nice drink of water and write down any notes or insights that you may have had during the process.

3. Feeling of competence at something.

Sit comfortably in a chair or on a cushion. Take a breath and let it out. Let your body feel the support of the chair. Take another breath and let it out. Begin to feel your diaphragm and solar plexus area. Take your next breath and take the breath in as if you were breathing deeply into your lungs. Bring the breath all the way down into the bottom of your lungs. Let your eyes close and let the feeling of your body just breathing wash over you. Now think about what you want to change. Keep feeling into the area of your diaphragm. As you think about it, run the description of change you wish to make through your mind and then see your solution going step by step. See each part working successfully. Then let your imagination go and see yourself happy and successful. When you are ready, bring yourself back. Take a final cleansing breath. Have a nice drink of water and write down any notes or insights that you may have had during the proces

> **ARE YOU DOING SOME SORT OF PHYSICAL EXERCISE EACH DAY?**
>
> **DO YOU HAVE YOUR BASIC NEEDS IN PLACE?**
>
> **DO YOU GET A CHANCE TO FEEL THAT YOU DID SOMETHING WELL, EACH AND EVERY DAY?**
>
> **IS THERE SOME SORT OF LOVE CONNECTION IN YOUR LIFE? (NOT SPECIFICALLY ROMANTIC LOVE)**
>
> **ARE YOU ABLE TO DO SOMETHING HONORABLE ON A REGULAR BASIS?**

4. SOME LOVE CONNECTION

Sit comfortably in a chair or on a cushion. Take a breath and let it out. Let your body feel the support of the chair. Take another breath and let it out. Begin to feel your pelvic area. Take your next breath and take the breath in as if you were breathing from your heart area. Bring the breath deeply into your heart. Let your eyes close and let the feeling of your body just breathing wash over you. Now think about what you want to change. Keep feeling into your heart and for a moment let yourself just love yourself. Then think about the change that you will be making. Allow yourself to be happy that you are making this change. Then just watch the images that flash by. Do not get involved with them. If your thoughts interrupt the images and the meditation and start to tell you negative things, stop the thoughts. Bring your mind back to your breath. Or you can begin to count your breaths. Allow yourself to see the change happening successfully. Let your imagination go and see yourself happy and successful. When you are ready bring yourself back, take a final cleansing breath. Have a nice drink of water and write down any notes or insights that you may have had during the process.

5. SOME LEVEL OF HONOR

Sit comfortably in a chair or on a cushion. Take a breath and let it out. Let your body feel the support of the chair. Take another breath and let it out. Begin to feel into your throat area. Take in your next breath as if you were breathing from your throat and let yourself make a small sound. Make a small hum or a sound on the exhale of your breath. Let your eyes close and let the feeling of your body just breathing wash over you. Now think about what you want to change. Keep feeling into the throat.

When you make the sound on the exhale, allow yourself to feel some joy. Then allow your mind to go blank for a moment and just watch what images flash by. Do not get involved with them. Just watch. When the images slow down, allow yourself to see the change happening successfully. Let your imagination go and see yourself happy and successful. Allow yourself to feel how honorable you are as a person. When you are ready bring yourself back. Take a final cleansing breath. Have a nice drink of water and write down any notes or insights that you may have had during the process.

6. COMPASSION WITH BOUNDARIES

Sit comfortably in a chair or on a cushion. Take a breath and let it out. Let your body feel the support of the chair. Take another breath and let it out. Begin to feel your forehead area. Take your next breath. Bring the breath gently into your lungs and let the tension go from your neck and your shoulders. Let your eyes close and let the feeling of your body just breathing wash over you. Now think about what you want to change. Keep feeling into the area of your forehead. Then just watch what images flash by. Do not get involved with them. Just watch. If you start to be overwhelmed pull yourself back a little into the now moment. Breathe and be. See and let go of what you see. When the images slow down, allow yourself to see the change happening successfully. Let your imagination go and see yourself happy and successful. Allow yourself the option that when you hold boundaries along with compassion you do not take away other people's opportunities for change. Instead you open up a space for them to grow into. When you are ready, bring yourself back. Take a final cleansing breath. Have a nice drink of water and write down any notes or insights that you may have had during the process.

7. LEARNING SOMETHING NEW

Sit comfortably in a chair or on a cushion. Take a breath and let it out. Let your body feel the support of the chair. Take another breath and let it out. Begin to feel the top of your head. Do not put a hand on it. Simply feel the top of your head from inside yourself. Take your next breath and take the breath deeply into your lung area. Bring the breath all the way down your torso. Let your eyes close and let the feeling of your body just breathing wash over you. Now think about what you want to change. Keep feeling into the top of your head. Let the mind go. Focus on the breath. Then just watch what images flash by. Do not get involved with them. Just watch. Think about what you want to learn and how you will accomplish that task and take another breath. Make the choice to learn all that you can. Make the choice to enjoy the learning process. Let your imagination go and see yourself happy and successful. When you are ready, bring yourself back. Take a final cleansing breath. Have a nice drink of water and write down any notes or insights that you may have had during the process.

> **ARE YOU ABLE TO KEEP HEALTHY BOUNDARIES WITH PEOPLE?**
>
> **DO YOU GET A CHANCE TO FEEL THAT YOU HAVE LEARNED SOMETHING EACH DAY?**
>
> **DO YOU GET A CHANCE TO PUT THAT NEW LEARNING INTO PRACTICE?**
>
> **DO YOU HAVE A REGULAR OPPORTUNITY TO DO SOMETHING ALTRUISTIC FOR YOUR FAMILY? COMMUNITY? THE EARTH?**
>
> **DO YOU HAVE SOME REGULAR EXPERIENCE OF SPIRITUALITY?**

8. INTEGRATING NEW INFORMATION INTO YOUR LIFE

Sit comfortably in a chair or on a cushion. Take a breath and let it out. Let your body feel the support of the chair. Take another breath and let it out. Begin to feel the area the surrounds your body. Take your next breath and take the breath in as if you were breathing from three feet above your head. In your next breath, bring the breath all the way down your body. Let your eyes close and let the feeling of your body just breathing wash over you. Now think about how you want to include your new learning in your life. Keep feeling above the head and breathing into your torso. Then just watch what images flash by. Allow yourself to see the impact that having this new and exciting information will create in your life. See your life change happening successfully. Let your imagination go and see yourself happy and successful. See yourself able to use this new information in positive ways in your life. If you like, you can see yourself writing a book or giving a lecture on the new information. When you are ready, bring yourself back. Take a final cleansing breath. Have a nice drink of water and write down any notes or insights that you may have had during the process.

9. SERVICE TO THE COMMUNITY OF THE EARTH AS A WHOLE

Sit comfortably in a chair or on a cushion. Take a breath and let it out. Let your body feel the support of the chair. Take another breath and let it out. Take your next breath and take the breath in as if you were breathing from your whole body. Bring the breath all the way down your body. Let your eyes close and let the feeling of your body just breathing wash over you. Then feel out of your body to the surrounding space. Think about the great tides of humanity and take the next breath. Now think about what you want to change. Keep feeling into humanity. How people breathe and move. How they long for connection and compassion. Then just watch what images flash by. Do not get involved with them. Just watch. Allow light to follow the breath and see that light flowing into humanity and the earth. Allow yourself to see the change you wish to support happening successfully. Let your imagination go and see yourself happy and successful when the change is accomplished. When you are ready, bring yourself back. Take a final cleansing breath. Have a nice drink of water and write down any notes or insights that you may have had during the process.

10. SPIRITUALITY

Sit comfortably in a chair or on a cushion. Take a breath and let it out. Let your body feel the support of the chair. Take another breath and let it out. Begin to feel your connection to all that is around you. Take your next breath and take the breath in as if you were breathing from your whole body. Let the breath flow all the way down your body. Let your eyes close and let the feeling of your body just breathing wash over you. Think a moment about your connection to all that is around you. Think about the beauty of the world and the potential it holds. And take another deep breath. Feel how good it feels to breathe. Now think about what you want to change. Allow yourself to see the change happening successfully. Let your imagination go and see yourself happy and successful. When you are ready, bring yourself back. Take a final cleansing breath. Have a nice drink of water and write down any notes or insights that you may have had during the process.

DO NOT HURRY THIS PROCESS!

It is not unusual in our society of fast food and over the counter drugs to want to fix things fast. You may have even tried the fast route already. For real change that is going to work in your life there are no fast fixes. With real change that has a solid effect in your life you make specific focused changes. Drinking alcohol can cloud the process of change. Taking medications that have not been prescribed can also interrupt the process of change. It can actually make the process of change take longer because it gives you a false sense of success. Taking alternative substances is a given way to sabotage the process of change as it actively affects your brain chemistry. Why start the process if you are going to guarantee failure from the beginning? Let yourself be successful.

IT TAKES DISCIPLINE, DETERMINATION AND COURAGE TO MAKE REAL CHANGES. YOU CAN DO THIS. SET YOURSELF UP FOR SUCCESS!

CHAPTER SIX

NEED FOR SUPPORT

When I was growing up, my riding coach shared with me some words of wisdom which I thought were very, very good. He said, "Don't set yourself up to fail. Set yourself up to succeed." If you do your planning in advance you can set yourself up and you are assured of at least partial success. There are times when everyone needs support. When you are engaged in a change process, you may need them more frequently than you normally do.

Sometimes information is what you need. Today, one can actually hire services that will do information seeking for you in your local area. For example, if you needed a new dry cleaner the service will actually go out and search all the dry cleaners for you. I pay my local folks about $35.00 an hour for them to do the research and they make the listing, give me the directions, tell me what the people include as services, what the people do not have as services available, specialized work, things like that. You get all that information and you don't have to spend the hours doing the research yourself.

Occasionally, one needs somebody to take practical actions to help you. For example, when my father passed away several years ago, his house needed to be cleaned before it was sold. It's hard to clean house from 3,000 miles away. So having somebody there to take practical actions to help you can be very, very important. There are times when some emotional support is what is needed. Sometimes you just need somebody to hear you and say, "Yes, you can do it." Just to hear you and be there for you. When I was doing transitions between graduate programs and I moved from one city to the next, my network was gone and it took me a little time to rebuild it. So I worked out a deal with one of my friends that I would talk to her once a week and I could complain all I wanted that one hour a week. She's another therapist. She said "no problem" and it allowed me to make the transition to start to get a support network in place.

You may need support because you are going on a physical journey though it actually can be any kind of journey. If you're traveling to Africa, for example, what kind of immunizations do you need? What kind of visas do you have to have? What kind of equipment do you want to take along? All of those things can be factors so any kind of a journey that you're involved in can be an issue.

It may be an end of life journey in which you are engaged. Getting the correct resources in place so that your questions are answered correctly and in a timely fashion can be very nurturing. Having your transition process prepared gives you less to worry about in the long term.

Sometimes you just need someone to use as an interested or disinterested sounding board. It can be wonderful to just having somebody listen, or somebody to hold a particular intent.

As I mentioned before, my daughter has chosen to be my "rah-rah" cheering section. She says, "You can do it, Mom" and I'm darned if I'm not going to succeed with her watching. So I set myself up so I will not fail, even though I don't like doing sit-ups.

Do not be embarrassed to ask for support. Instead take action for success!

WHAT ARE SOME OF THE POSSIBLE TYPES OF SUPPORT YOU MAY NEED SO THAT YOU CAN BE SUCCESSFUL?

INFORMATION CLEARING HOUSE.

SOMEONE TO TAKE PRACTICAL ACTIONS TO HELP.

EMOTIONAL SUPPORT.

CLARIFICATION ON THE STEPS TO TAKE IN AN END-OF-LIFE JOURNEY.

INTERESTED/DISINTERESTED PARTY TO USE AS A SOUNDING BOARD.

SOMEONE TO HOLD A PARTICULAR INTENT.

CHAPTER SEVEN

INTERNAL AND EXTERNAL RESISTANCE

What are the challenges that you're going to face as you start to make changes? The biggest is your internal self-resistance. Your body is a chemical/electrical system. If you focus on the electrical part of the system for a moment you will be focused on the nervous system. Each person has a certain level of wiring in their nervous system. In the same way you'd get static on a cell phone or static on an electrical line, you can get static in the electrical system of the body. That static is another name for resistance.

> **WHAT ARE THE CHALLENGES YOU WILL FACE AS YOU MAKE CHANGES?**
>
> **INTERNAL RESISTANCE INCLUDING SELF-DISCIPLINE.**
>
> **EXTERNAL RESISTANCE IN YOUR ENVIRONMENT.**

Resistance may show up in a number of different physical ways. Internal resistance can appear as sore muscles. It may show up as sorrow. It may show up as becoming very emotional. It may show as a need to be in a place where you can be quiet and cry, or where you can laugh, or giggle at the oddest moments.

If you take the resistance that appears as a roadmap and as confirmation that you are changing, it can be a powerful tool. Start with the recognition that resistance has appeared. It translates to "I've made a change! Let resistance be a bell that rings to say, "I'm being successful," instead of "Oh, this is so hard; I can't do it." Allow yourself to reframe your need to cry or rage or pace or be frustrated and use it as a barometer of where you are. It can be very, very valuable and it helps keep your self discipline moving in the right direction.

WHERE DOES RESISTANCE COME FROM?

YOU ARE CHANGING THE FREQUENCY RANGE OF INFORMATION AND EXPERIENCE AND WHERE THEY ARE STORED IN THE BODY.

You can also have external resistance in your environment. Your change in your body can produce external resistance in your environment. That resistance comes from a change in frequency range where information and experience are stored in your body and it acts much the same way as static does on any kind of electrical wire. You can inadvertently trigger old defensive patterns. Physical, verbal, emotional and belief patterns, it causes a change in current flow in the nervous system as you start to hit these areas of resistance. It's a marker of success that you're making the change.

> **AN OLD DEFENSIVE PATTERN, BELIEF PATTERN OR HOLDING PATTERN GETS TRIGGERED. (PHYSICAL, VERBAL OR EMOTIONAL)**
>
> **THIS IS CAUSED BY ELECTRICAL CURRENT FLOW WHEN AN INCREASED CHARGE IS PLACED ON THE SYSTEM AS IT FLOWS A NEW WAY.**

When those moments hit, if you can recognize them as sign posts and allow them to simply pass, you will be supporting the progress of change. You can use them as markers that you are making good progress. Allow that moment, that possibility of change. It is a really, really important step toward your success.

CHAPTER EIGHT

POSSIBILITY OF CHANGE

As you change your life, one of the very first things that you are going to hit is internal change. When it hits, you will get to practice self discipline at a whole new level. It is not an easy process to create a system of change because you fight yourself as you make the change. I cannot stress strongly enough the need to put as many supports in place as possible so that you can make and maintain the change you are longing to make. Doing the thinking, planning and putting those supports in place is powerful. In the process of hitting your own and others' resistance to change you must give yourself permission to change. The act of giving yourself permission to make the change is often as powerful as the change itself. The act is an act of empowerment.

In addition to your internal resistance you can have external resistance in your environment. When I started back to graduate school I had to be at school in the evenings, and my husband at the time had to do a lot of cooking, babysitting and overseeing homework when he had come home from 10 hour days and was tired. He was wonderfully supportive and he did it, but it was hard on both of us. So there was external resistance in my environment, largely because we were both exhausted.

One of the options to help you in the change process is to understand why you are making the change and what you gain from making the change.

For example: when I exercise regularly, I may ache all over but in the long run I lose weight and reduce the stress on my heart.

> **WHAT DO YOU GAIN BY MAKING CHANGES?**
>
> **WHAT DO YOUR FAMILY OR FRIENDS GAIN IF YOU MAKE THE CHANGES?**
>
> **HOW DOES YOUR WORK SITUATION CHANGE IF YOU MAKE LIFE CHANGES?**

Take another minute and see if you can answer the questions listed in bold. It helps to know why you believe this is a necessary change. Again, this is one of the supports to help make that change process happen more smoothly. You need to be sure it is the correct change to make and you need to know why you are making this specific change.

Equally important as knowing why you are making the change is to understand what will not change when you fail or do not make the change that you are longing to make. This is the dark side of the change process. If you try, you can convince yourself that you really do not need to make the changes that will improve your life. Things may be working almost well enough that it is just more effort to go ahead and make the changes you long to make. It is true that the process of change may be stressful on your family and your friends. It is true that as you change, your job may not fit you as well as it once did. It is true that you will be a different person tomorrow because you have made the change you were longing to make.

> **WHAT DO YOU GAIN BY NOT MAKING CHANGES?**
>
> **WHAT DO YOUR FAMILY OR FRIENDS GAIN IF THINGS REMAIN THE WAY THAT THEY ARE?**
>
> **DOES YOUR WORKING SITUATION REMAIN THE SAME IF YOU DO NOT MAKE CHANGES?**

Again, take a few minutes and answer the questions listed above. When you know what the issues will be, you can put support in place to make the change process easier for everyone.

One of the options you have in the change process is allowing yourself to pick the right time for you to begin. Let yourself have a little give and let your life have a little give so that you pick the time to start when you are prepared and organized.

Think about what you gain in making the changes. Stay focused on the gain once you start. You know a healthier, happier you is going to positively affect everyone around you. Everybody from your best friend to your cousins to your aunts, uncles and your children or if you are not at the child stage yet, whoever you are connected with, good friends in your life, your working environment, all of those kinds of things can change. Everyone around you will gain as you become healthier.

Remember that you want to do things to help yourself stay positive and stay focused. Have a cheering session. Do the advanced planning. Set yourself up to be successful. Remember that thought has weight so when you hit a point where you are talking about the changes that you are making, listen to the words you are using. Are they words that are going to support you? Remember to say, I am really excited about this. I think I can do it. I feel like I can do it. I am sure that I can do it.

CHAPTER NINE

ADVANCE PLANNING

When you begin to implement your life changes, advance planning becomes critical. If you plan correctly, your changes can happen with a minimum of fuss. If you plan correctly, you will have the resources that you need to make your changes. If you plan correctly, you will not have to fail. In the long run you have to work harder to fail because you will be putting more energy into resistance and into the negative processes in your life.

There are a number of factors to consider in your advance planning process. Begin with the time you will spend planning, implementing the change and actually doing the new behavior. These also include the language which you use on a day to day basis to describe and dialogue about the change you will be making. How the changes will affect your family, friends and even your work situation. Whether or not you expect support or resistance from family members in response to the changes you will be making. Noticing if you are creating a situation where family responses become the excuse for you to fail in your change process. Seeking out the necessary information to accomplish the changes you wish to make. And finally, planning time for integration of the change and to just be still and experience the new you. These are all part of the advance planning process.

SELECTION OF WHICH CHANGE TO MAKE

PLANNING, IMPLEMENTATION, AND THE DOING!

There are four basic steps to the process of change. The first is sometimes the most difficult. It is the selection of which change you wish to make. Pick just one to start. Most people try to make too many changes all at once and just cannot coordinate the process. Pick one thing you wish to change and have it be something simple.

The second step is the actual planning process. In this step you will break the change process into bite sized pieces. Who will be making the change? That will be you. What change will you be making? This will be based on which of the daily needs you want to work on. Remember to keep your first change simple and focused. Why are you making this change?

The first possible reason is because it will help you to be healthier. The second possible reason is because it will help you to be happier. But what are your exact reasons? Why is making this change important to you? Understand why you believe you need to make the change and what your goal is in making it. It will help you be stronger and more focused as you make the change. Remember you want to set yourself up to be successful.

Where and when will you be making the change? Will you be exercising by dancing to music in your living room three times a week? Will you be learning a new language by going to a class at your local community college two nights a week? Design a schedule that you can actually live with not one that is a dream. If you are taking a class and you have children, who will watch them?

How will you handle it if someone is sick? How will you arrange your time so that you can study? Think all of these questions through carefully.

The third step is the implementation of your changes. Have you gotten your baby sitter all lined up? Have you registered for your class? Have you signed up for the gym and made the process of paying for it each month easy? What steps need to be in place to make you successful? What day will you start your change? Set your target goal for beginning the process and go for it!

Finally, how does this change feel? Are you enjoying the experience? Does your body feel better after a month into the new process? Are you starting to feel more positive about your life? Check in with yourself and give yourself a pat on the back for doing a good job! Pick something to reward yourself with that is life supporting. Go to a movie with friends. Make a fun dinner. Go dancing with your significant other. Getting started with the first change is the most difficult in my experience. Once you have the method down the sky is close at hand.

WHAT INFORMATION DO I NEED?

Finding the information you need to make a change can be an important step in the process. There are information services that can help you find information. You can go to the library or to the book store to find information. You can contact businesses that are relevant to the change you want to make. I had lovely conversations with people at three different gyms when I decided that a gym membership was what I needed to help me exercise more regularly. Try looking on the web. You can usually get a range of information and lots of business names through that process. Contact your local Chamber of Commerce for information. Learn about the change you want to make. Spend time in research. It will help make the change process smoother. Remember to set yourself up to be successful by careful research, planning and organizing.

Language and the Process

Remember, thought has weight so when you hit a point where you are talking about the changes that you are going to make, listen to the words you are using. Are the words that are going to support you? If you are saying to your friends and family, "Oh I am never going to be able to do this," such self-defeating language can make it more difficult. If you are instead saying, "I have started this. I am really excited about this. I think I can do it. I feel like I can do it. I am sure that I can do it" this will help support and sustain you and will reinforce your behavior and your changes. While positive thinking alone is not enough, since you must also take action, positive thinking and mastering your mind and its language provides you with solid reinforcement of your change.

Look at the specific words you are using. Also check into yourself. When you are talking about the process, do you feel a kind of tug on your heart or a sense of disbelief or untruth as you speak the words? When you are saying how you are feeling, how you are doing things, do you feel kind of a tug on your heart? Is there something in the process that just whispers to you that you will not be successful? You know, very often when we start into something new it does not work exactly in the way we have envisioned it and we need to tweak things just a little bit. You will want to give yourself space to tweak things if necessary. If you feel that tug on your heart or a tug between the words, something that is just not quite working correctly, remember that you can take advantage of just a little more time, reorganizing, or refocusing. This is a very, very important piece to do.

FRIENDS AND FAMILY

Change can be difficult for those around you. You are a different person than you were yesterday. People around you will often need time to catch up to the new you. Because you are different you will take actions and say things differently than those around you might expect. You may have a different schedule. You may be less available because you are engaged in study. You may be getting more fit and people are noticing!

> **LISTEN TO THE WORDS YOU USE.**
> **NOW LISTEN BETWEEN THE WORDS**
> **— WHEN DO YOU FEEL A TUG ON YOUR HEART?**
>
> **REMEMBER THAT EMOTIONAL RESPONSES**
> **HAPPEN FASTER THAN THOUGHT**
> **AND WHEN A PERSON IS IN PAIN THEY SAY**
> **THINGS THEY REGRET LATER.**
>
> **FORGIVE YOURSELF AND FORGIVE THEM!**

Because you are changing it will affect all of the people who are regularly in your life. You will release energy in a new way. They will respond in a new way. Often in the release process, emotions will be more on the surface. People in your life may feel as if they are less in control of the environment and the situation in which they find themselves. Be patient with yourself and with those around you.

Remember that emotions happen faster than thought and when you are in those periods of static release, that extra energy that the body is holding can cause a major emotional response.

Remember those emotional responses can happen faster than thought. If someone says to you in that state or if you say certain things to someone in that state, take a breath, refocus, reorganize yourself and think about how you would really want to say something. Then go back. If you need to clean up a mess that you have made because you have responded too fast, do so. Forgive yourself, forgive the other person. Have a dialogue about it. Make good contact with the other person that you had the exchange with and get clear on what you want to say and how you want to say it. It is very, very important to continue to communicate well in this process.

WORK AND THE CHANGES

Sometimes work is the change you want to make and sometimes the change you want to make affects your work. If you want to walk every day at lunch and in the past you have always worked through lunch it may be a very direct change. Did you know that people who exercise during the day at work are more productive? It is good for your body and good for the business in which you work. But it may be a surprise to your co-workers. Be prepared to explain what you are doing and why. You might inspire those around you.

If your change is looking for a new job, be sure to make the change in a reasoned and careful way. Research and be fully prepared for the steps you will be taking as you make the changes in your career.

RESISTANCE TO CHANGE
Family can provide friction in the process of change but so can the feelings inside you. If you have done your planning well your transition process will be easy and relatively smooth. But there can always be bumps in the process. Check in with yourself if you start to experience those bumps and begin to feeling frustrated or defeated. How are you resisting making this change? More important, why are you resisting making the change?

Then do some thinking about how you might ease your own resistance to the change process. Is it something very practical? For example, if you are achy after you exercise do you need to schedule a massage once a week? Do you need to go to the drug store and get something to help your sore muscles until they get stronger? Do you need to modify the exercise program and go a little more slowly? Make a choice to problem solve instead of resisting the change.

INTEGRATION, DE-INTEGRATION AND THE NEW YOU
In the process of planning your selected change, be sure to add in some integration and de-integration time. Integration time is when you experience the changes in your body. You

may get an emotional response such as satisfaction for being able to follow through on your change. You may simply feel better all over. You may feel that you can move forward in your life in a new way and find that you are thinking and planning your next change.

De-integration time is just hanging out. Maybe you like reading a book. Maybe you enjoy just sitting on a porch swing and watching the world go by. I love to sit on my porch swing in the evening and watch the sky change as the sun is setting. I love to listen to the changes in bird song as they settle in for the night. I love to hear the quiet of the evening steal over the desert.

Most people do not schedule any time in their day to just hang out. It is good for the body to spend a small amount of time each day that is unscheduled and unscripted. In your brain there are some very important chemicals. One is norepinephrine, which is the fight/flight chemical. It allows you to respond rapidly to situations in which you might find yourself. The other is serotonin. It is a feel-good chemical. The body needs time to relax or what is called down regulate the chemistry between norepinephrine and serotonin so that you brain can work in a way that is healthy. So be sure to schedule some length of time to just hang out as you make your changes.

Advance planning can help you make the changes you want to make. It can help you meet the daily needs of your body. It can help you to be successful. Take a little time in the beginning to do your planning and you can smooth out the process of making your desired changes.

CHAPTER TEN

NO GUILT – THE RESTART!

One of the big challenges in the change process is that change can be hard, hard, hard. The logistics, the time, the family and life upheaval can all make change a challenging process. It often looks as if it can be easier to stay stuck and just not have to deal with the fallout in your life when you are in the middle of the change process.

First, you need to recognize that is the stuck part of yourself talking. It wants to stay stuck. It will give you all the reasons why you cannot make or keep the change you are making. It does not tell you the truth. It tells you the information that is stuck in your body system.

Second, if you are hearing this part of yourself complain, you are making progress!!!! It means that you have hit your areas of resistance. Give yourself a pat on the back and then tell the complainer inside the self to be quiet. It is not telling you the truth. It just needs a little more push to move things and change things. Do some thinking about what you can do to help yourself move through this part of the change process. Do you need to tune the process? Do you need to trim down the amount of time that you are spending doing the new activity?

Change can also be scary when you step into being a more powerful, capable, self-determining individual. Part of being a healthier individual is discovering what you need and like in life.

Who is this new and happier you? One of the challenges that people have as they change is that the people who are around them change as well. Are the people in your life supporting your development or are they limiting you in some way? Can you dialogue with them and share the direction in which you wish to move? Or are you beginning to develop new friends that have similar interests and a similar focus? Let yourself grow into who you are becoming. It is a great person!

What can you do if you cannot keep up the changes that you have made? Most important you do not want to go around and feel guilty. My mother who was a psychiatrist said to me once, "you know, guilt is a useless emotion unless you use it to move yourself forward in a positive way."

Do not spend any time feeling guilty if you cannot make everything work the way you had originally planned. Take a big pause, retune the situation. Look at the process with fresh eyes and start fresh from that moment. If you absolutely, positively have to have your guilt, use it for a moment to help spur you forward and then make a fresh start, make a new change, then go ahead and start back into the process with a fresh attitude and a good starting place.

Begin your fresh look by spending an hour or two and focusing on what part of the change process is working and what part is not working. What kind of planning and changes might you need to make to help you move forward? Do you need some sort of external support? Do you need more information? Do you need to create space in your life in a different way so that you can make the change work? Once you have isolated what is and is not working begin problem solving. Walk through the steps in the book again and tune the process so that you can become successful.

Each moment in life can be a fresh start if you choose to live that way. You are a different person today than you were yesterday. Who do you want to be today? How do you want to be different? Can you identify a new direction for your life? Let yourself be a new and fresh person and discover how rich and joyous your life can become.

> **WHAT CAN YOU DO IF YOU CANNOT KEEP UP THE CHANGES THAT YOU HAVE MADE?**
>
> **DO NOT SPEND A MOMENT OF TIME FEELING GUILTY.**
>
> **INSTEAD MAKE A NEW CHANGE AND START FRESH!**

CHAPTER ELEVEN

THE NEXT DAY OF YOUR LIFE

Are you ready to start becoming a healthier and happier person? Start today! Do your planning and pick one aspect of your life on which to start your change. Plan what you are going to change and how you will change that one thing. How are you implementing the process? Do you have the correct support in place to allow yourself to be successful? Ask these questions and get your support in place.

Begin the process of implementing your change tomorrow. Take one step at a time. Review your progress on a regular basis. Check in! Do you need to modify your goal? Do you need a different kind of support? What has the impact been on your family? Do they need support or dialogue?

Is the change effective? Are you feeling better, stronger and as if your life is moving forward? Have you made the change in a way that you can put the change into regular practice in your life? Do you need to tweak things at all so that they change can be part of your life and be life supporting? Give yourself permission to be successful. You can make the changes that you need and move forward in your life.

The world provides you with options and choices if you choose to take them and make them. Remember to analyze your situation, check and see if you are meeting your daily needs, do your planning, make your changes and then become the person you wish to be.

WELCOME TO THE NEXT DAY AND THE NEXT PHASE IN YOUR HEALTHIER AND HAPPIER LIFE!

ABOUT THE AUTHOR

MELINDA H. CONNOR

Beginning her training as a child in the energy skills, she is the founder of Earthsongs Holistic Consulting & Executive Director of the International Journal of Healing & Caring. She is the lineage holder for the Resonance Modulation energy skills training program. Between Harvard, Wellesley, University of San Francisco, California Coast University, University of Arizona, American Military University and seminary programs, she holds three master's degrees and two doctorates.

Dr. Connor was trained in research as an NIH T-32 postdoctoral fellow in the Program in Integrative Medicine from the University of Arizona. Professor Connor is the former chair of the board of directors for the National Alliance of Energy Practitioners and is also both nationally certified by NCCOEP and board certified by the American Alternative Medicine Association.

She is a lifetime fellow of the Royal Society of Medicine in the UK, professor emerita and former research director at Akamai University, and the author of ten books. Professor Connor has received both international awards from *CEO Today Magazine* and *Finance Monthly* and US recognition from the *California State Legislative Assembly*. Named a top research scientist by the World Qigong Congress and Marque's Who's

Who, she was recently bestowed with the prestigious title of Empowered Woman of the Year for 2024 by the International Association of Top Professionals (IAOTP). This recognition is a testament to her outstanding leadership, unwavering dedication, and unparalleled commitment to the industry.

WWW.DrMelindaHConnor.com
WWW.EarthSongs.com
WWW.IJHC.org

www.ingramcontent.com/pod-product-compliance
Lightning Source LLC
Chambersburg PA
CBHW071729040426
42446CB00011B/2276